Pattern Coloring Pages

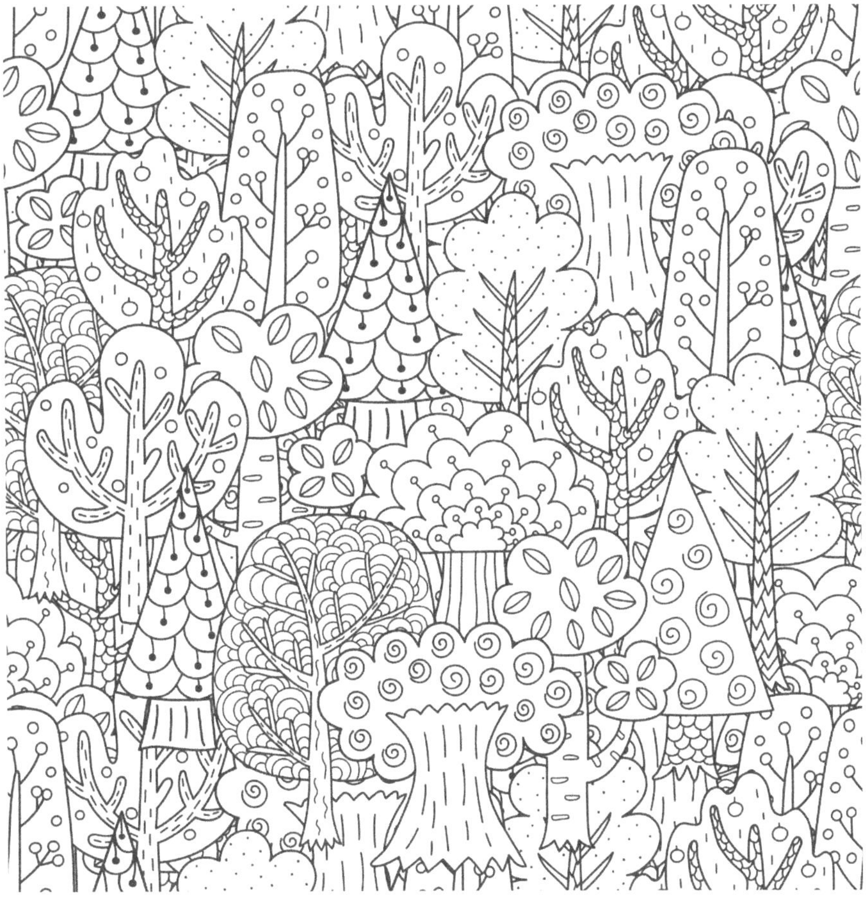

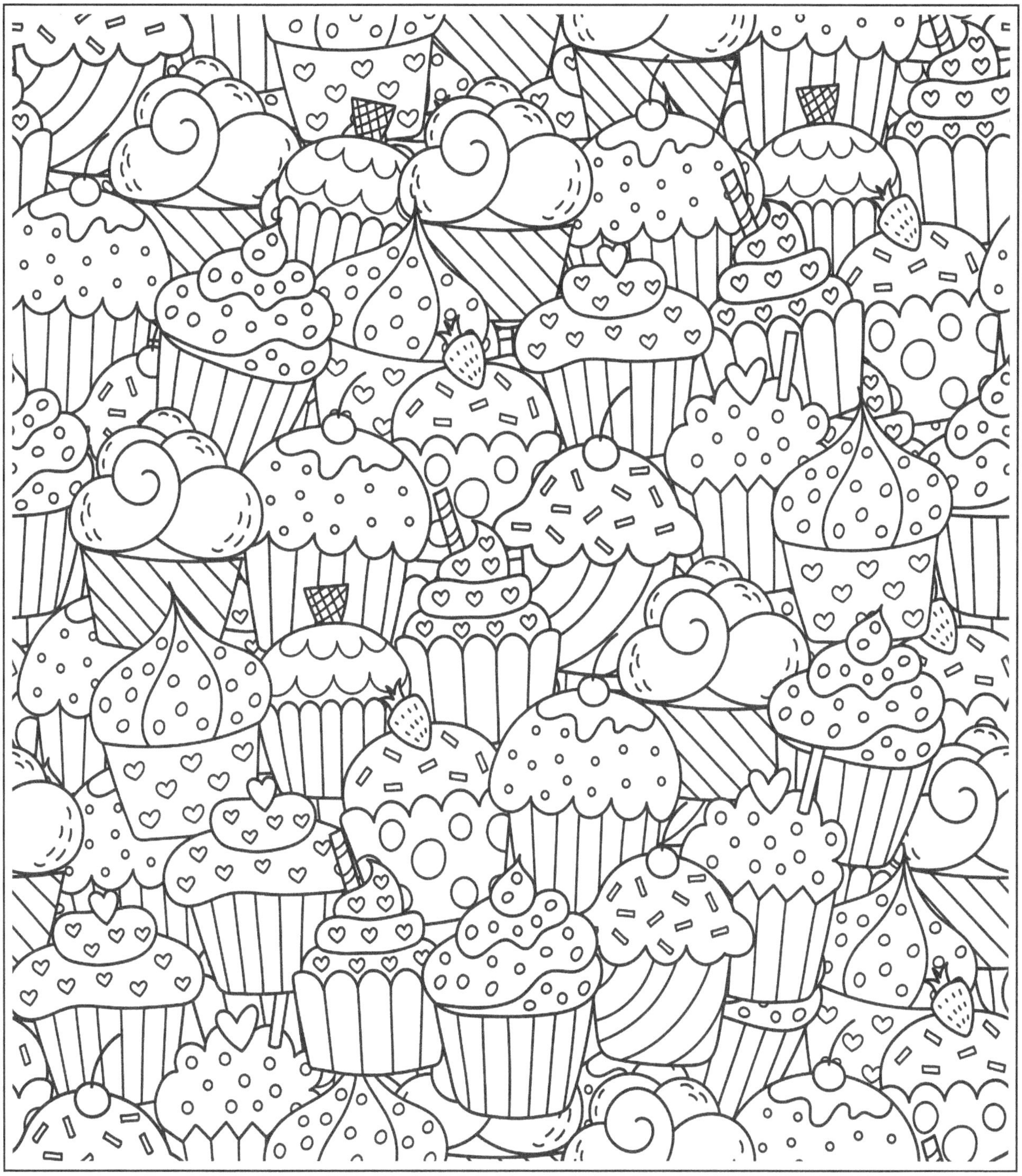

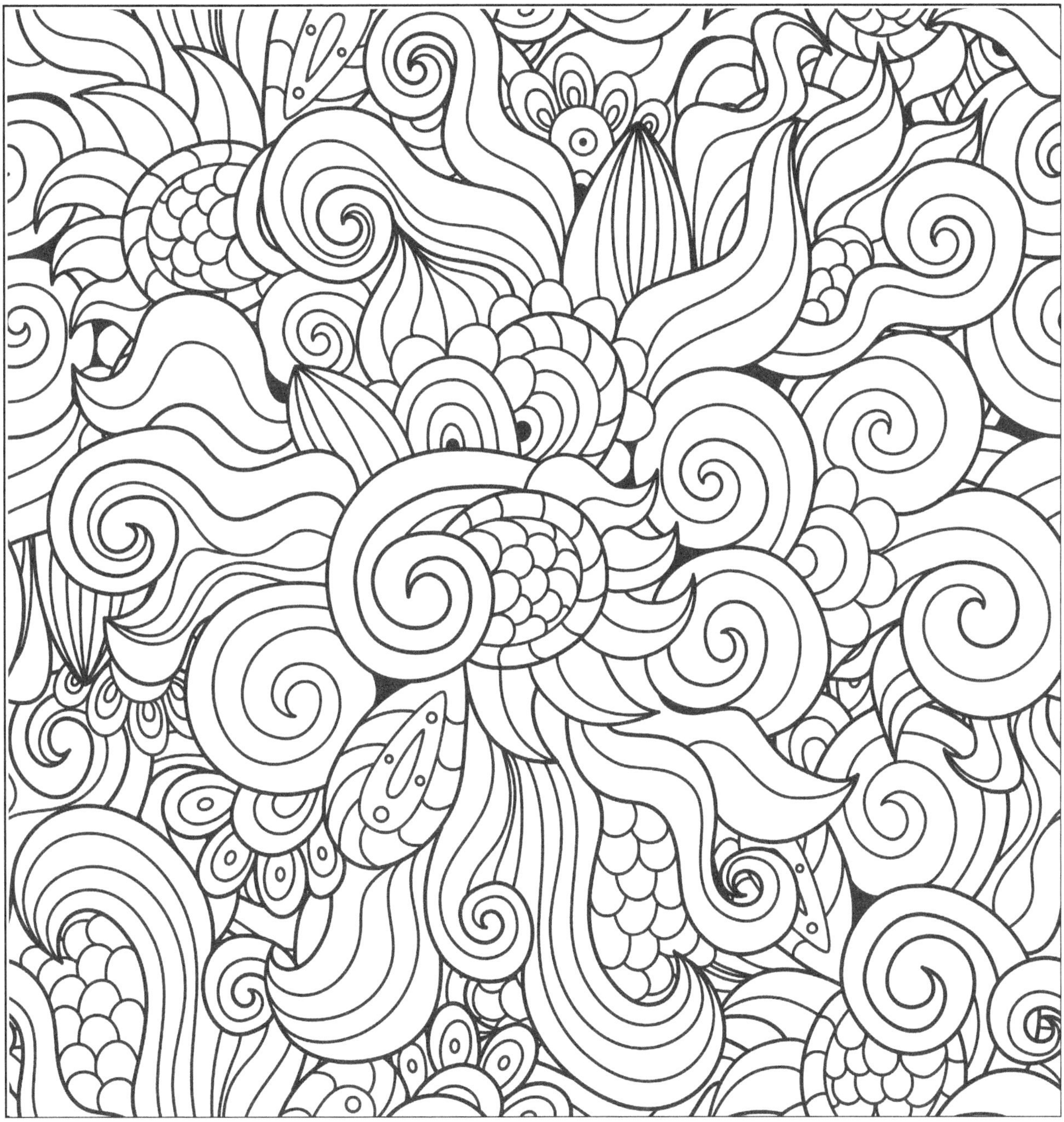

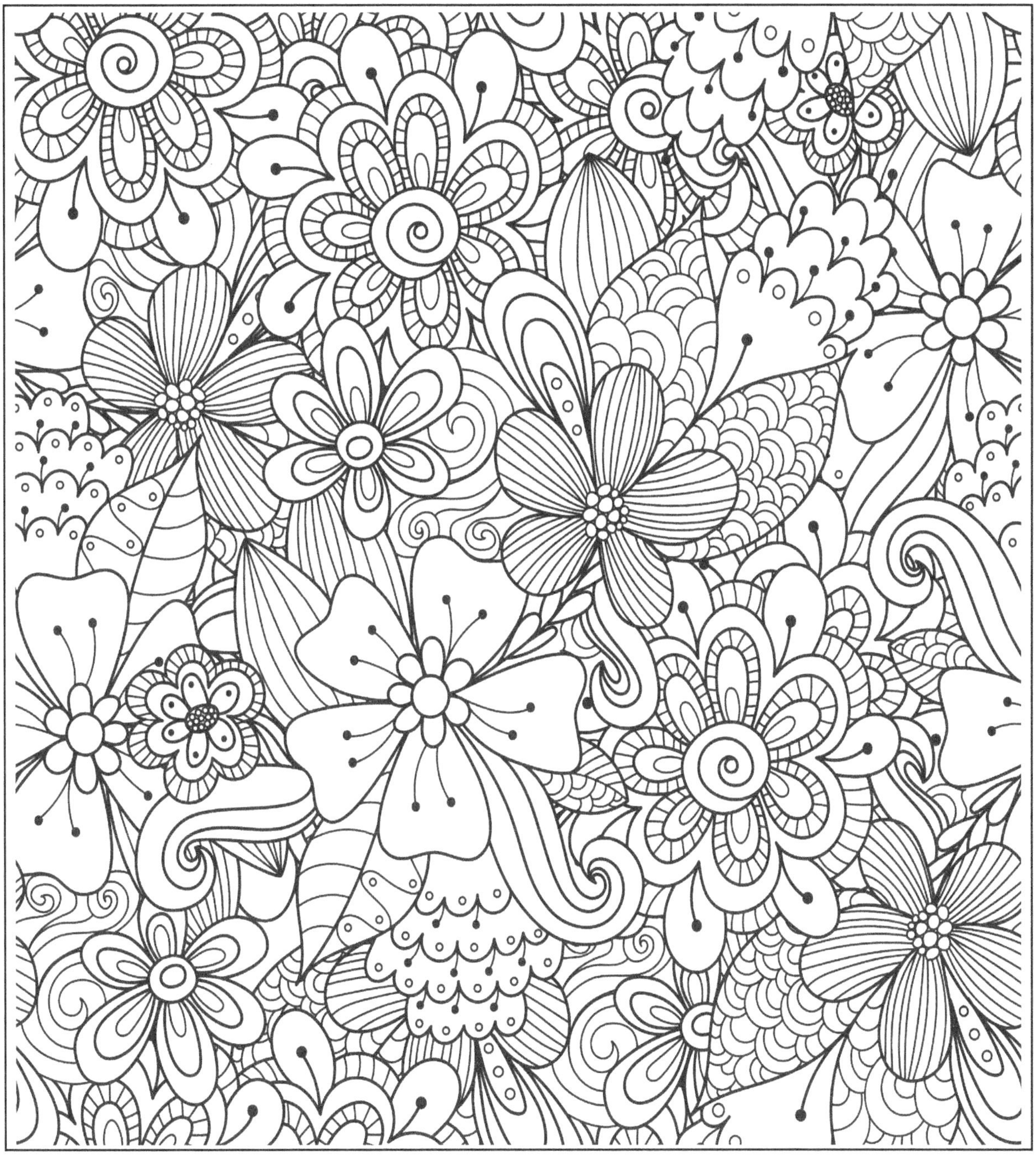

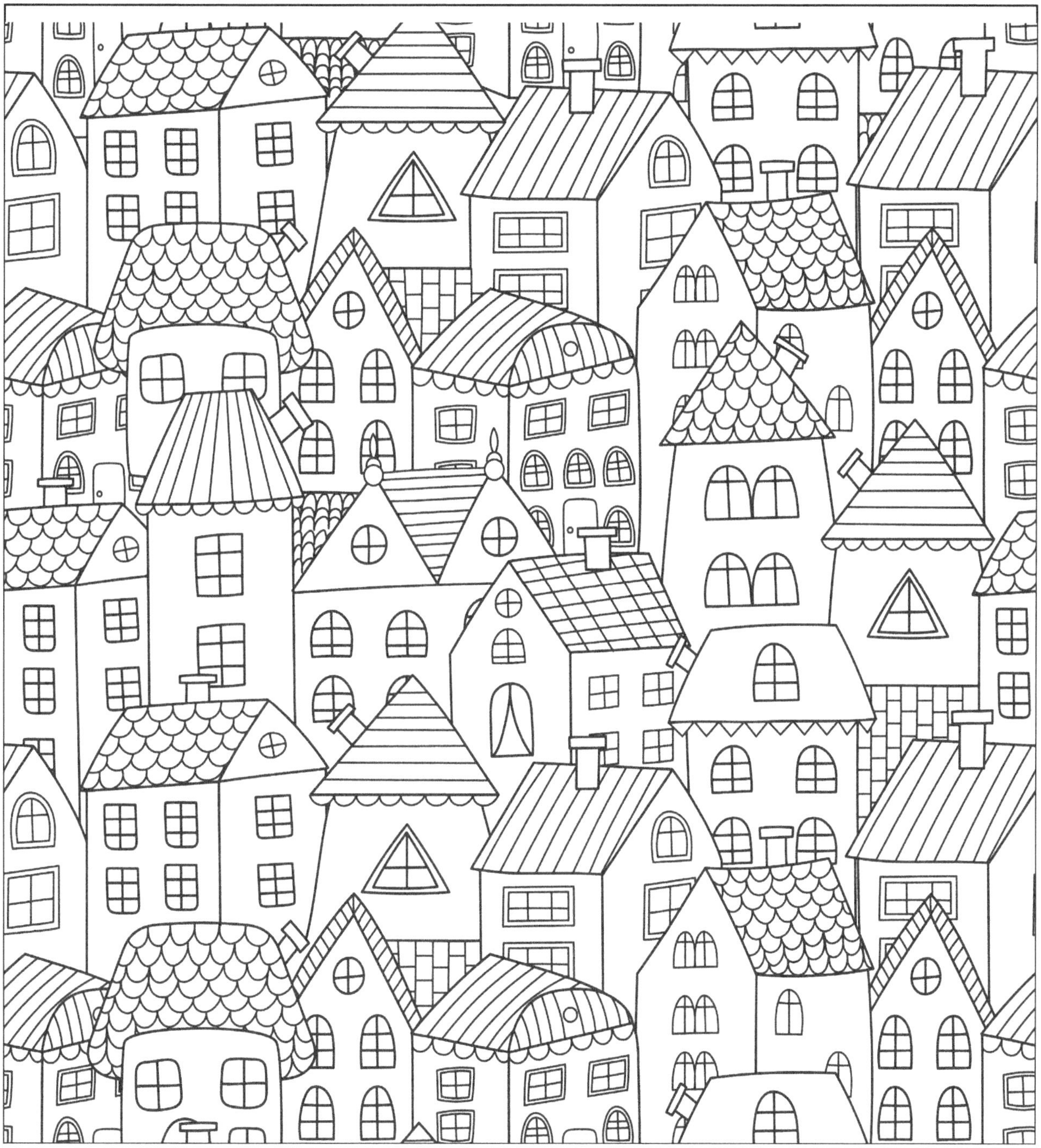

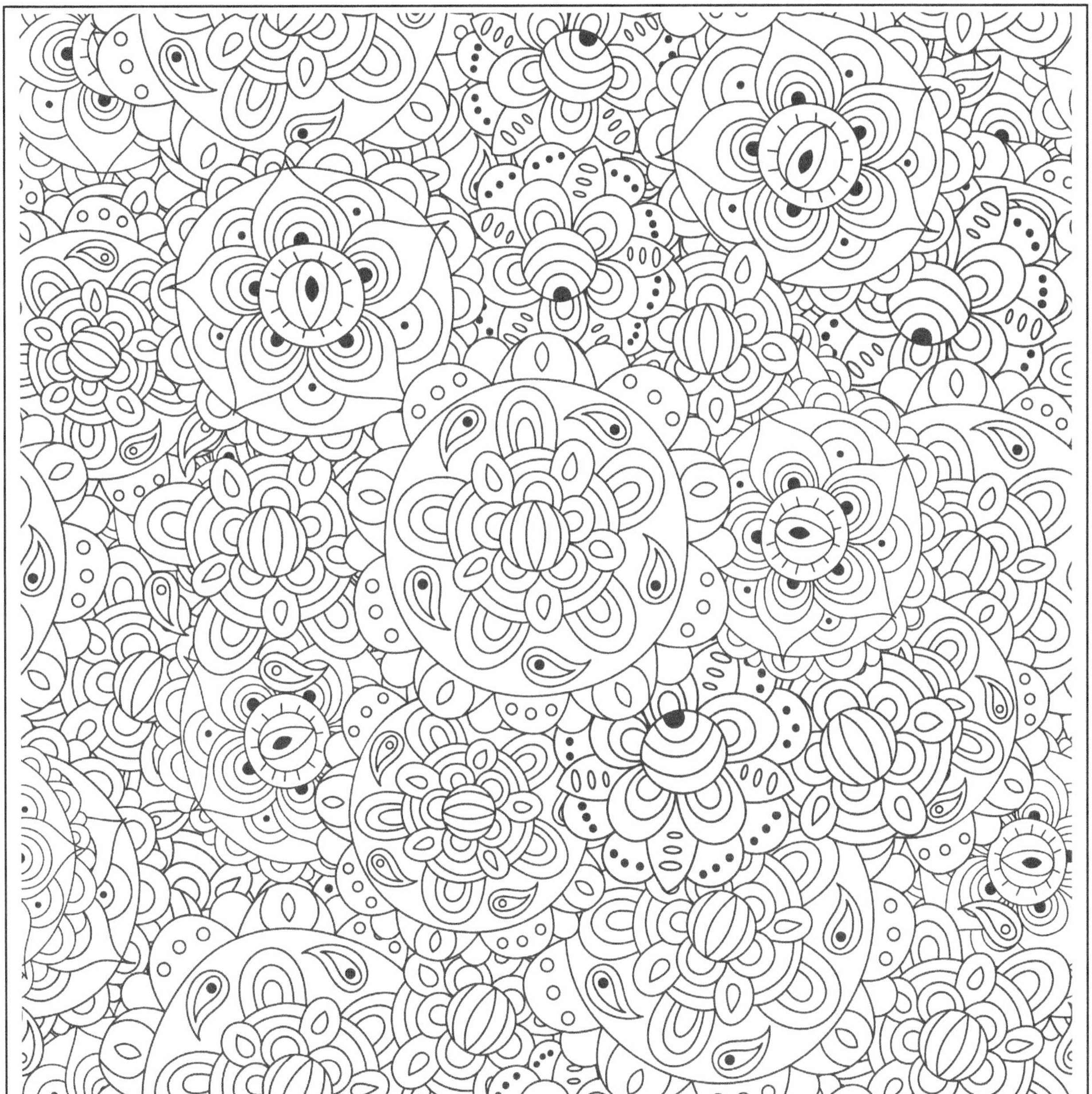

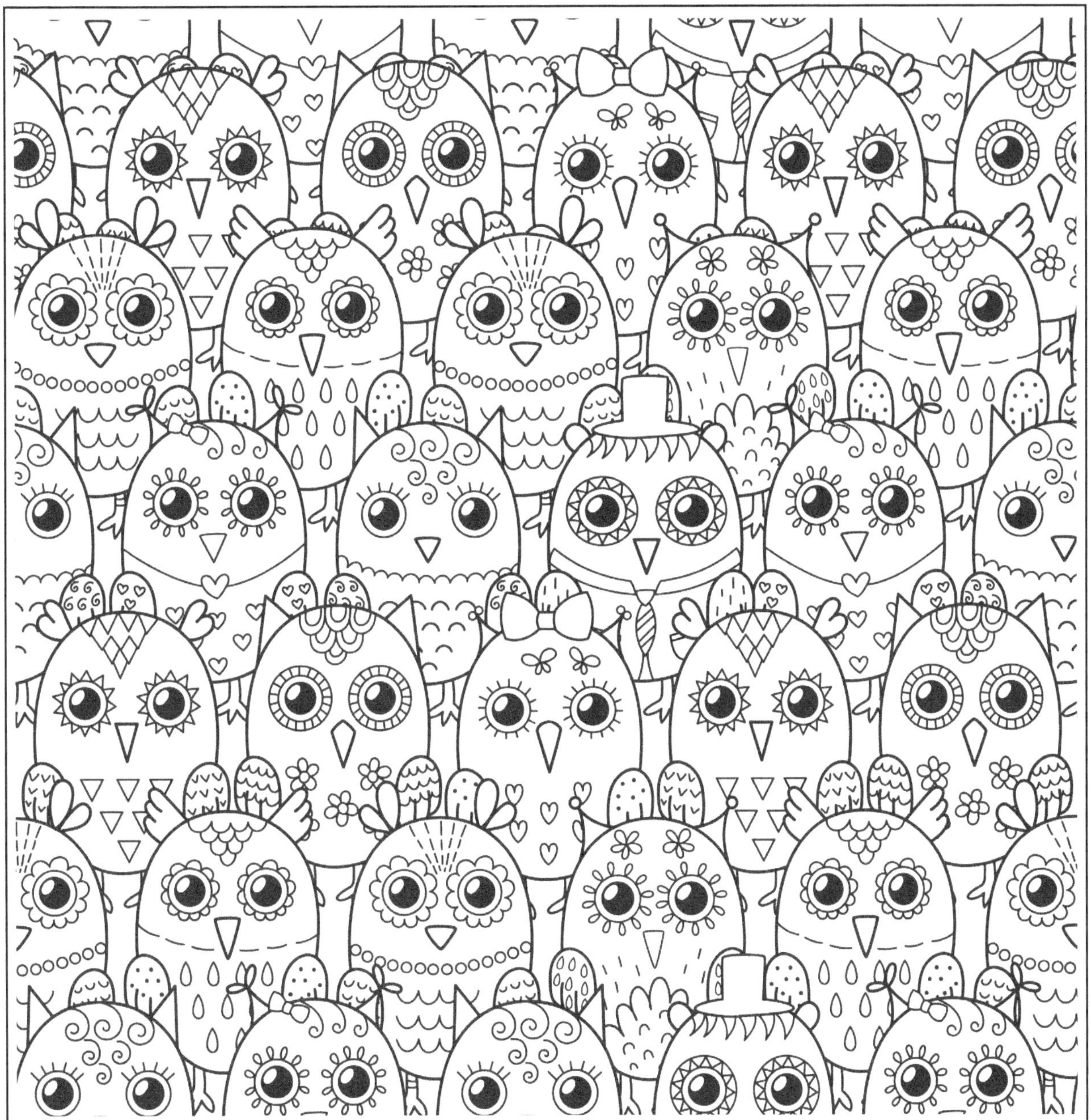

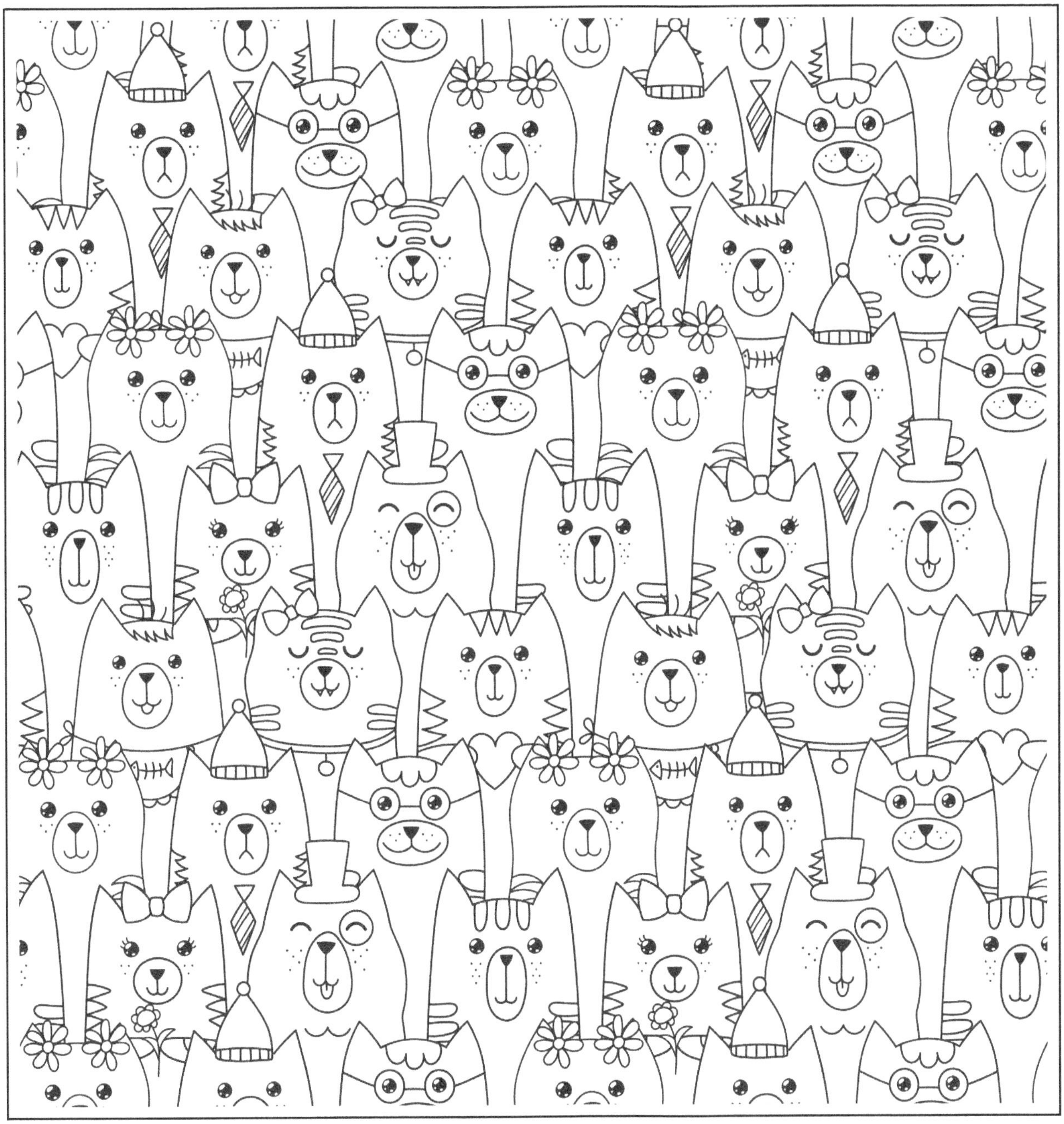

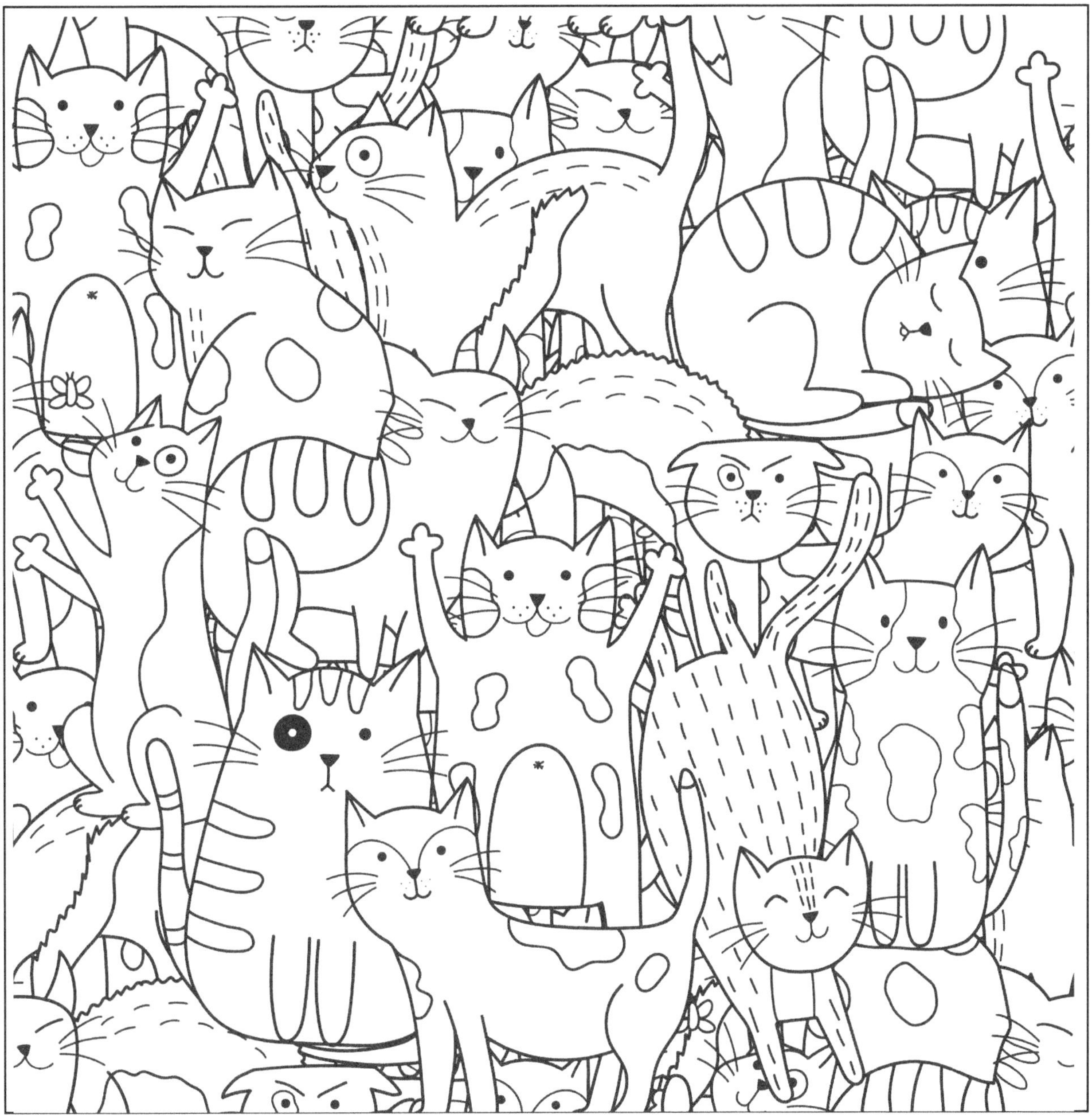

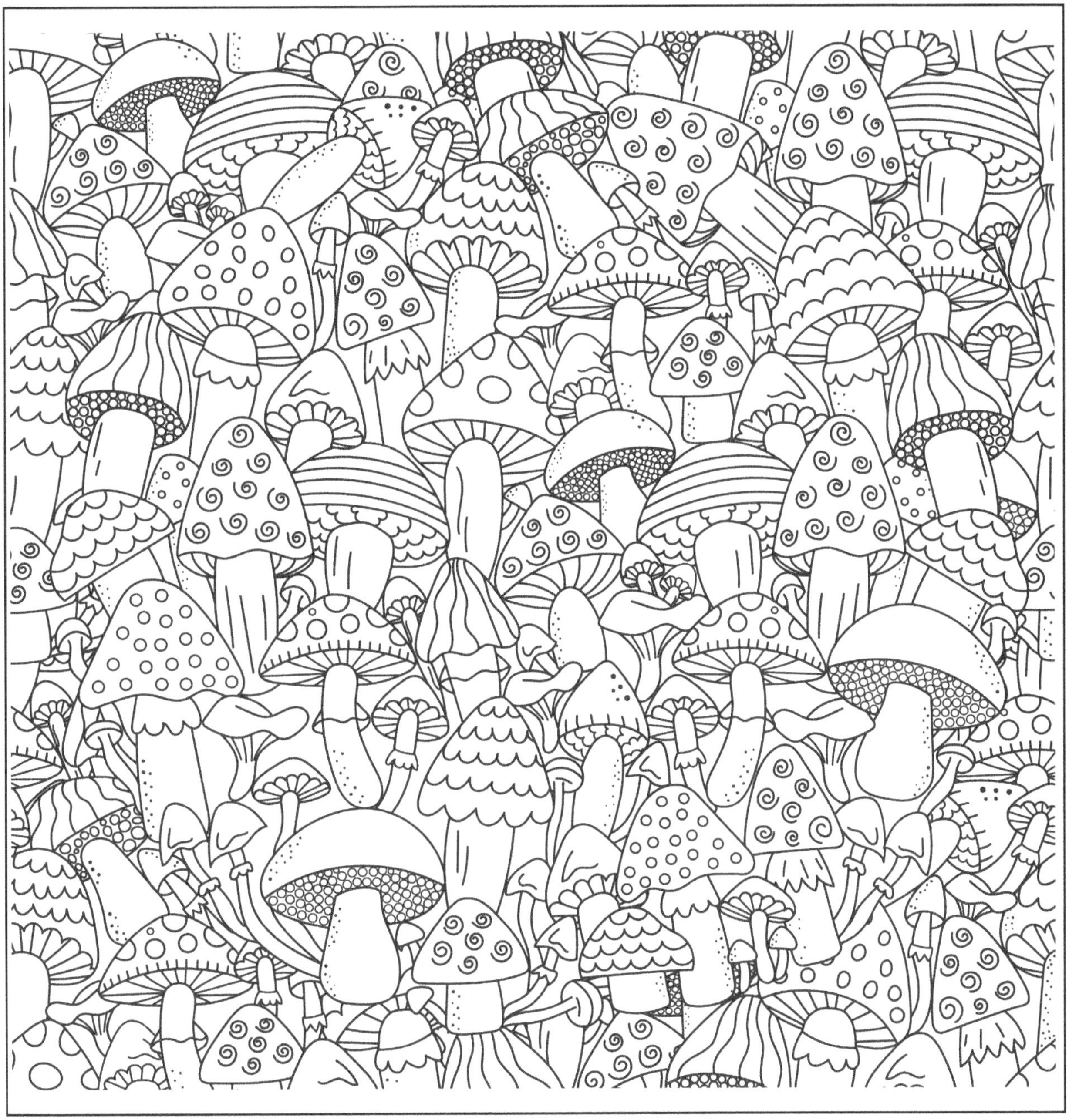

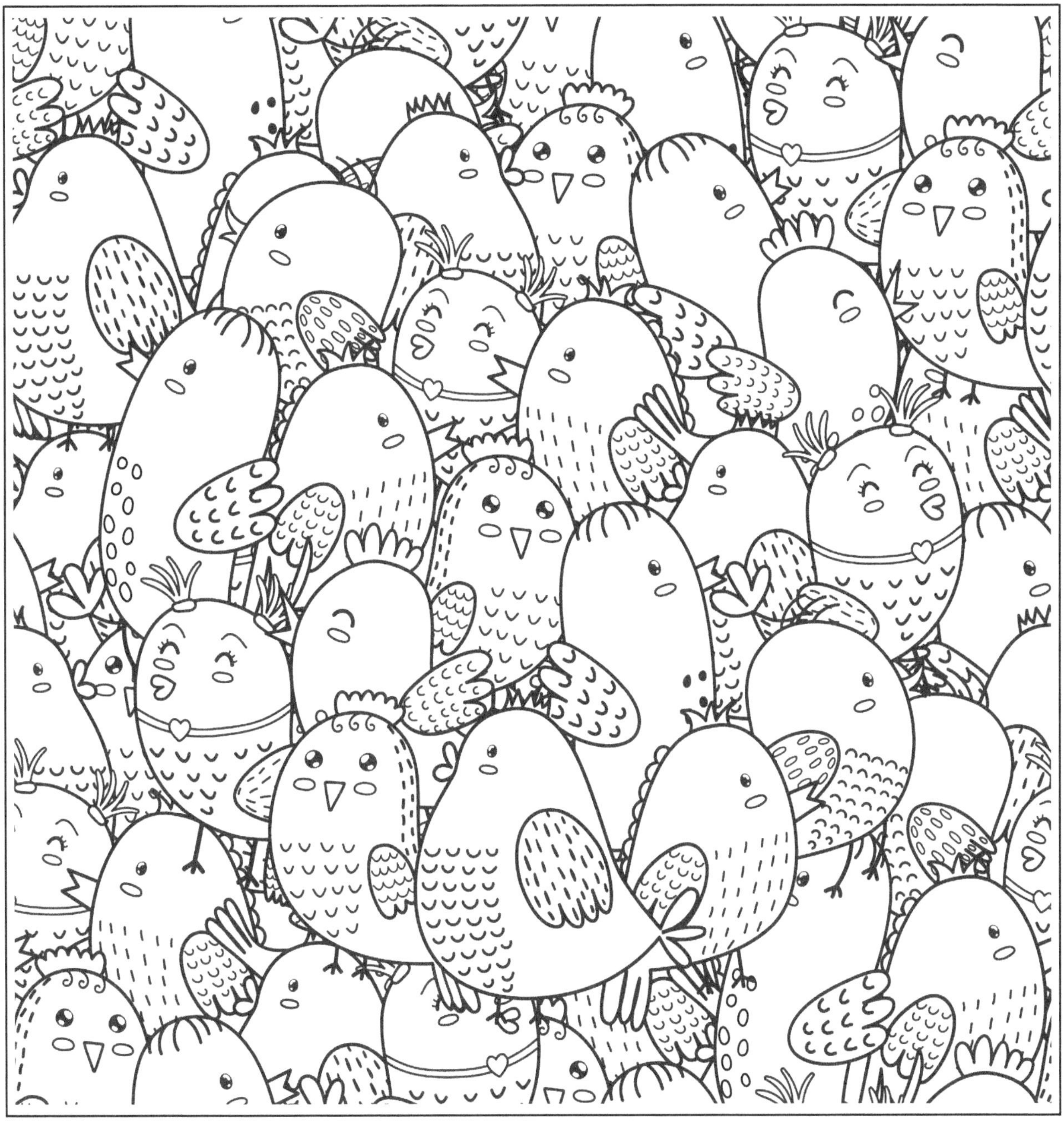

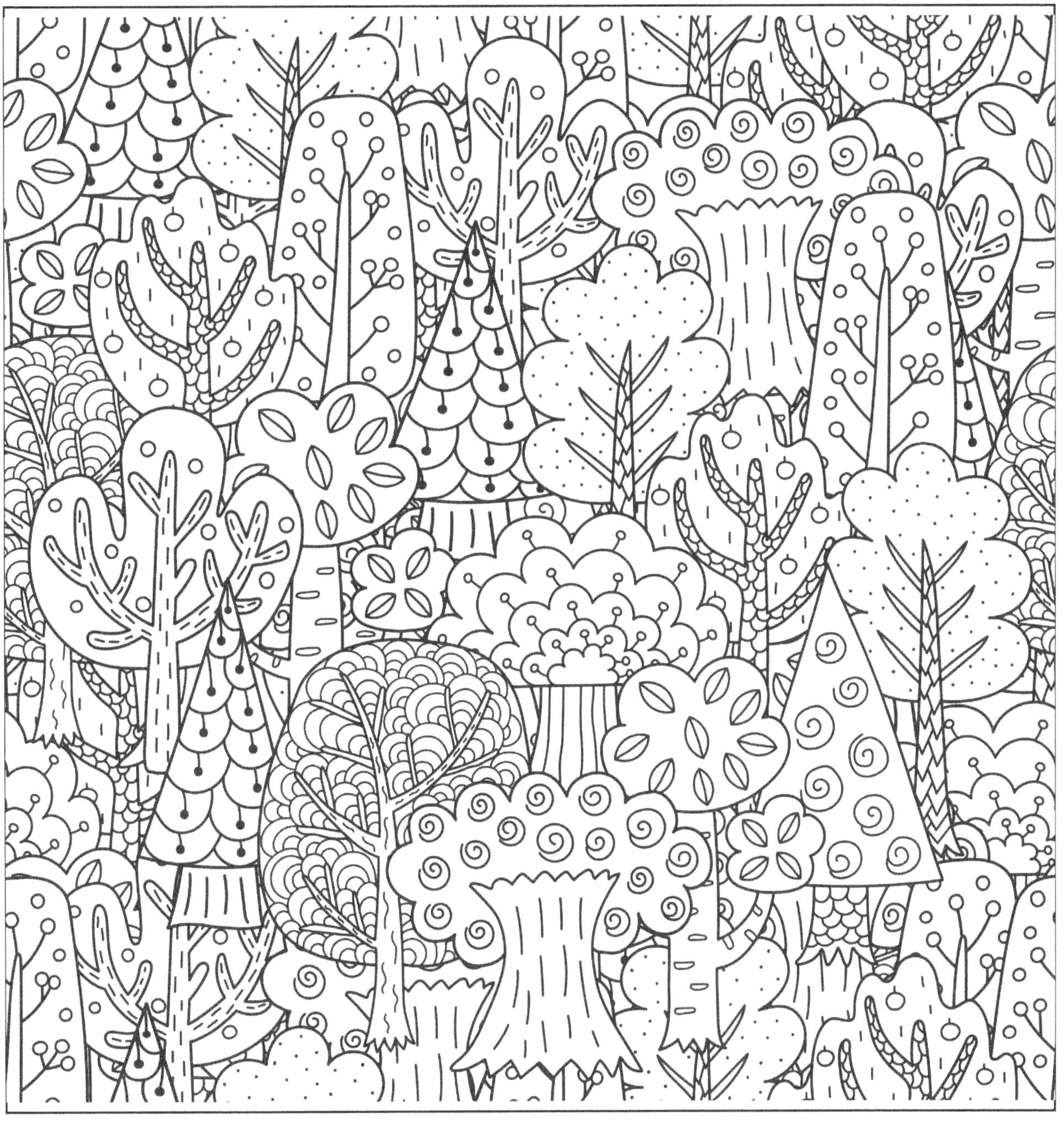

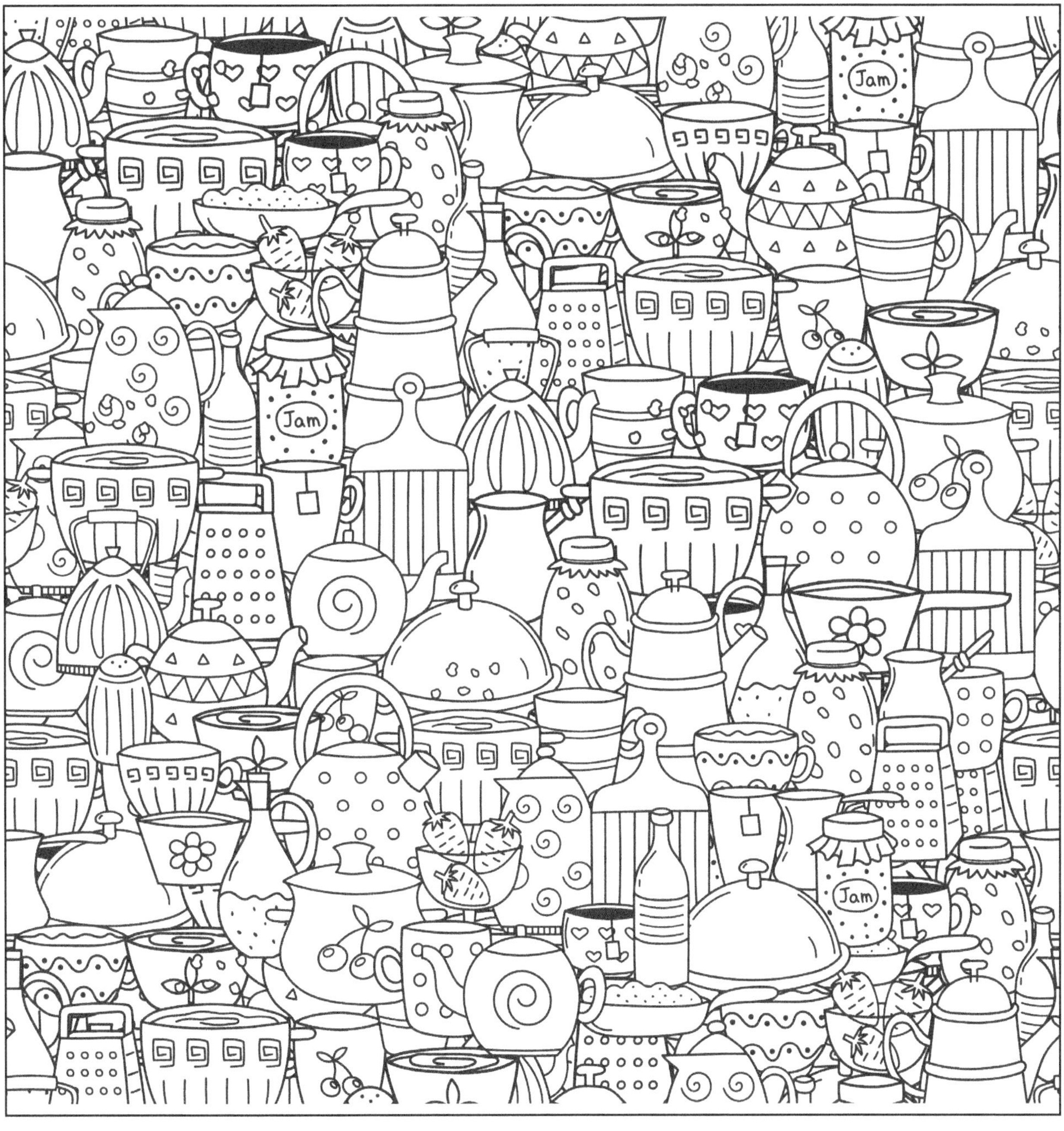
Jam
Jam
Jam

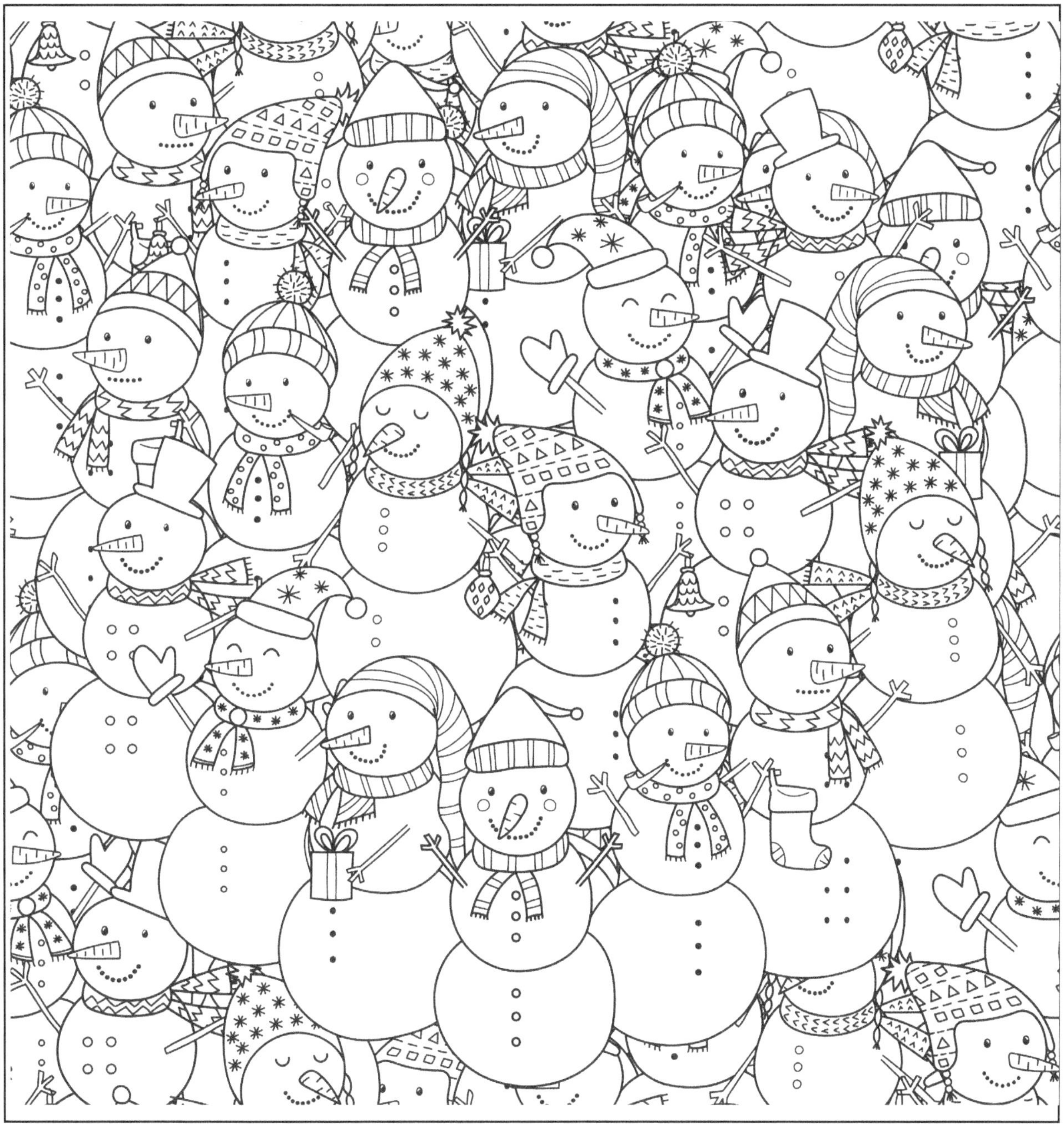

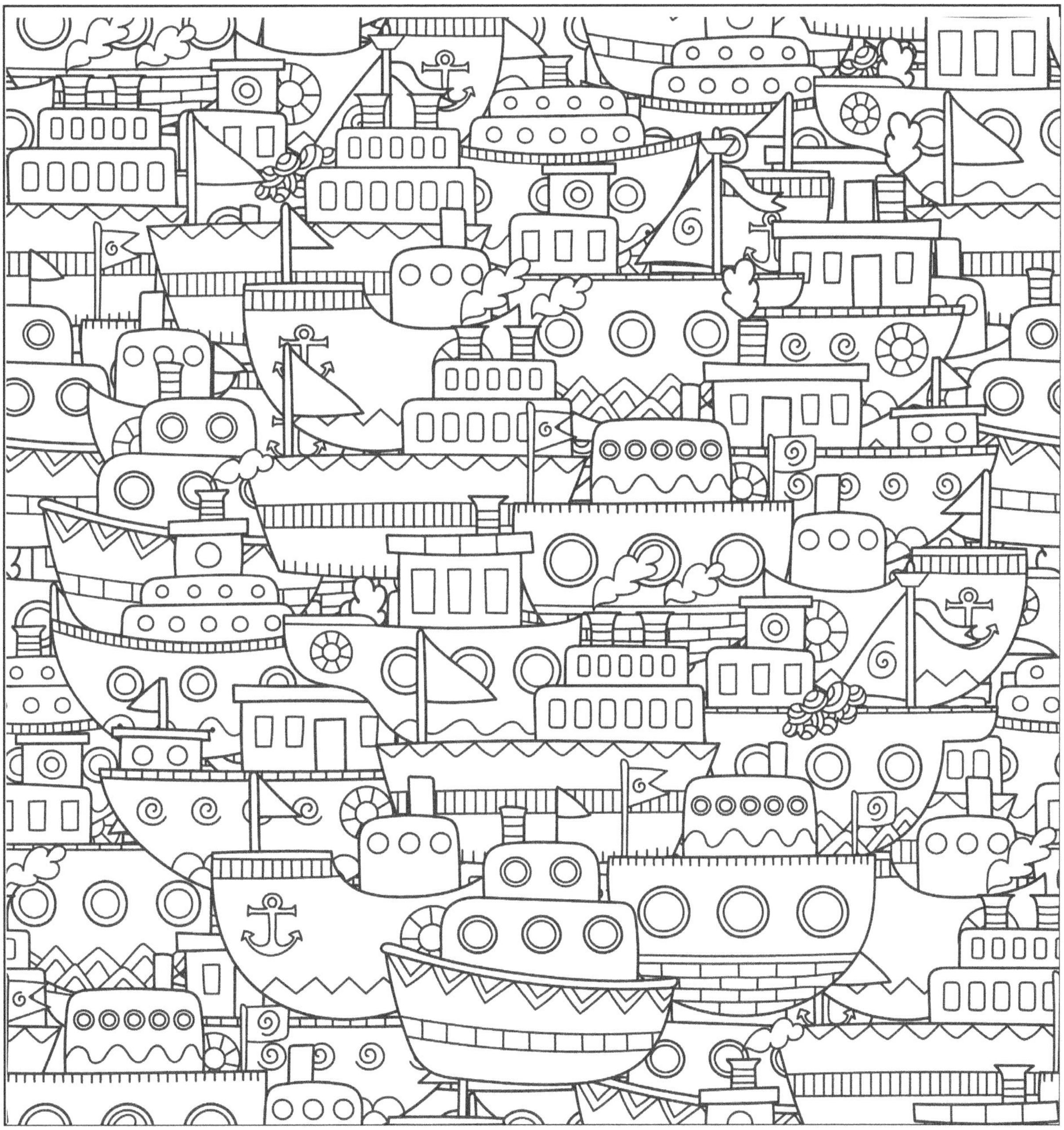

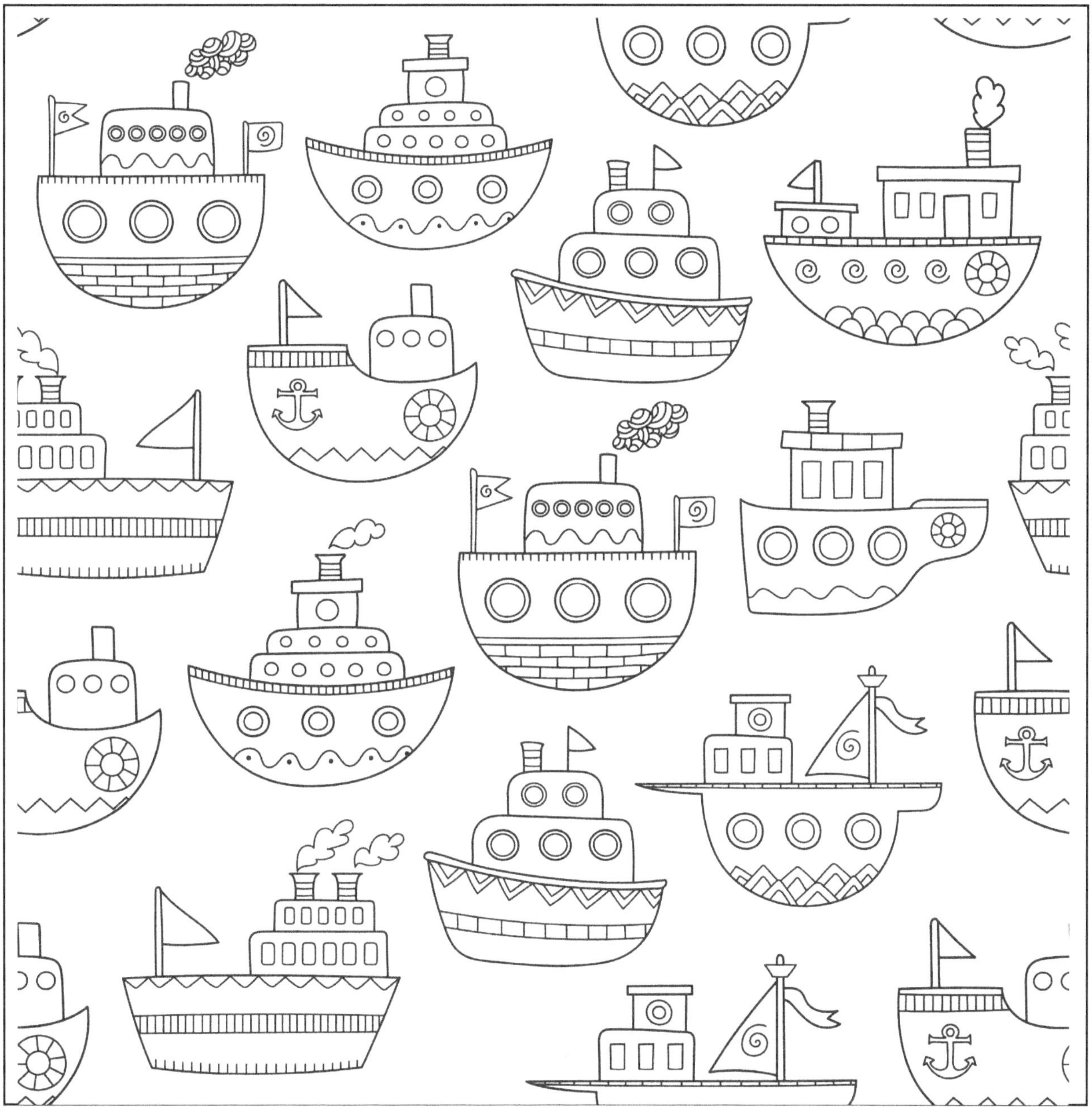

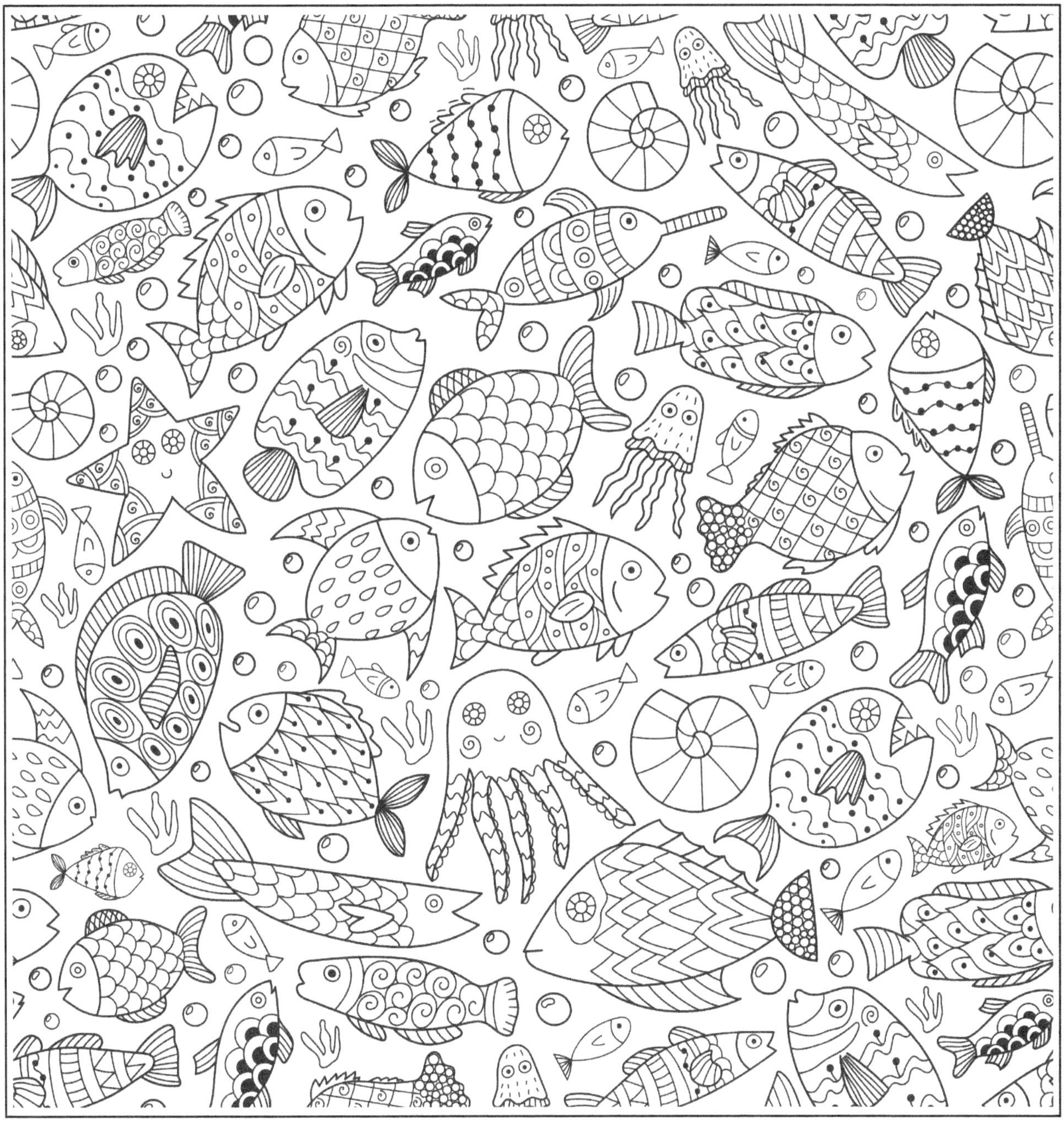

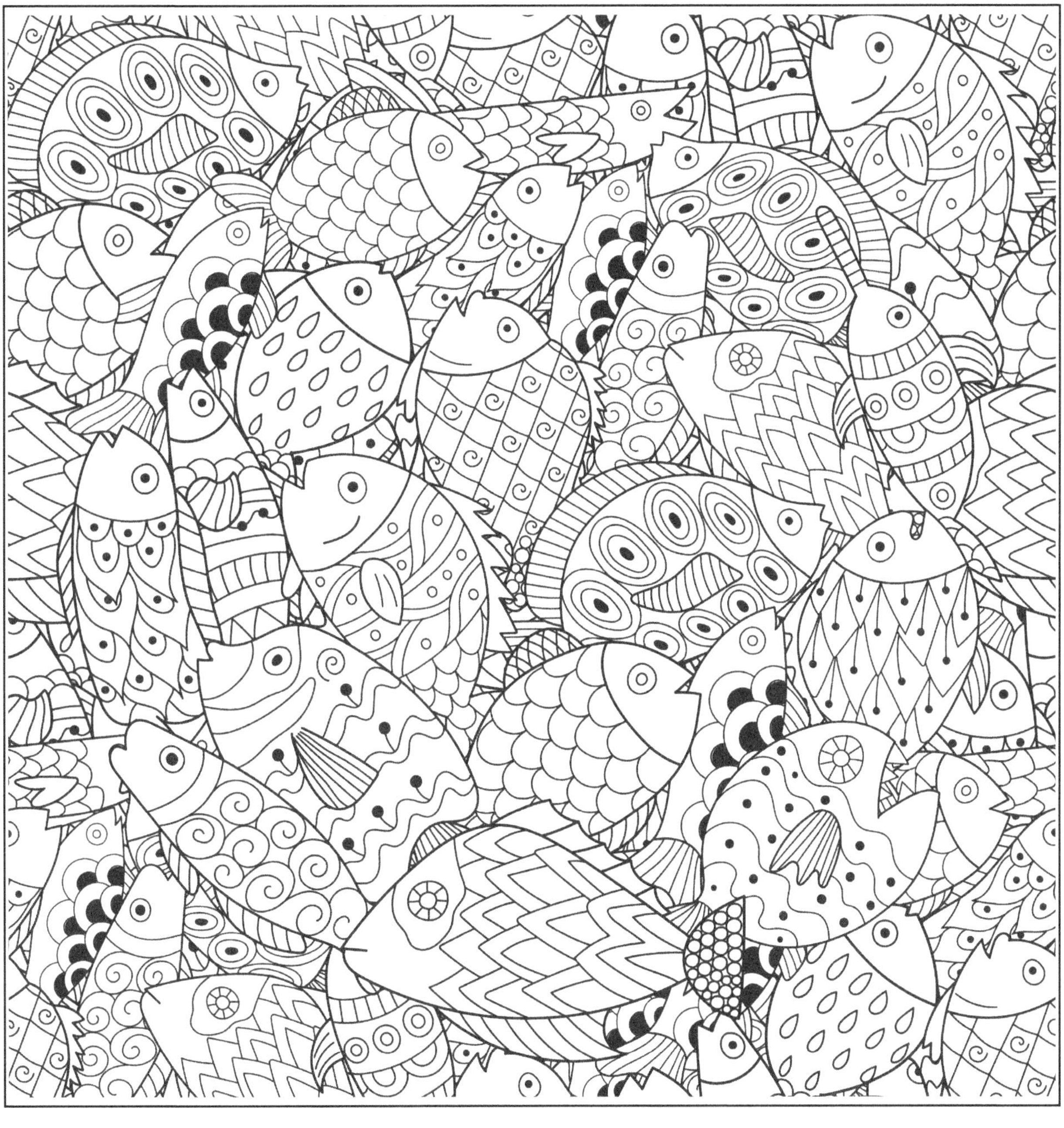

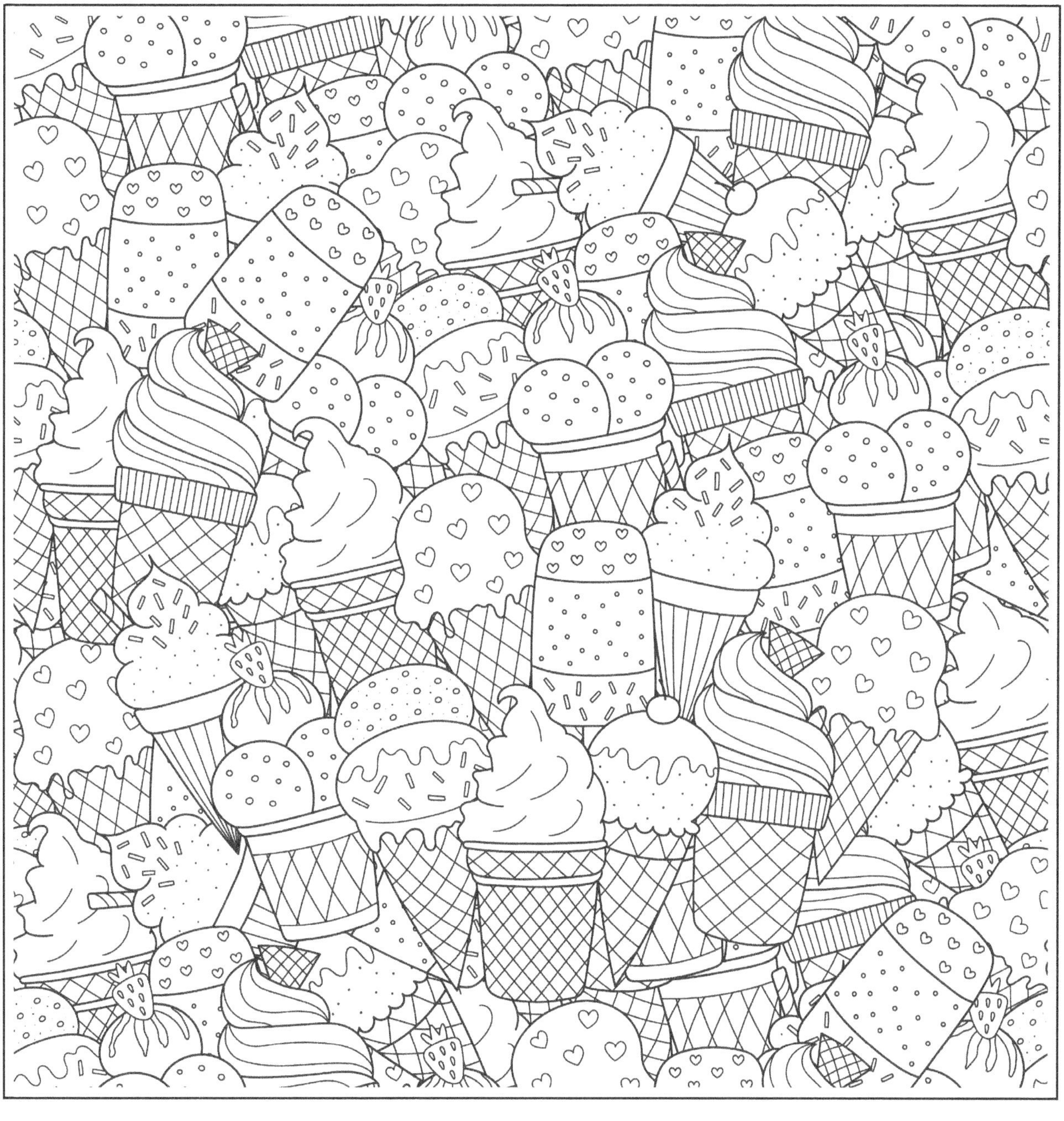

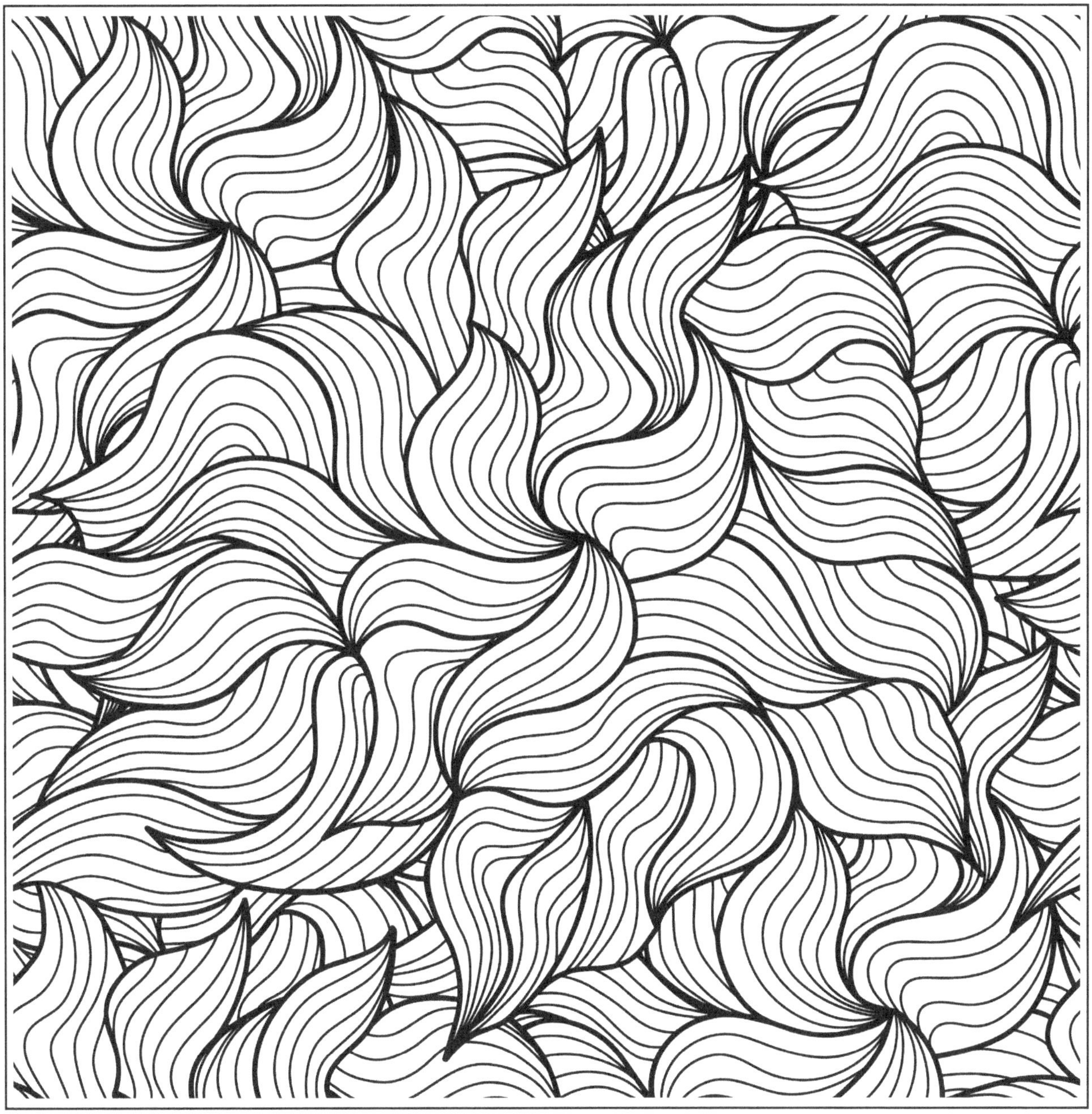

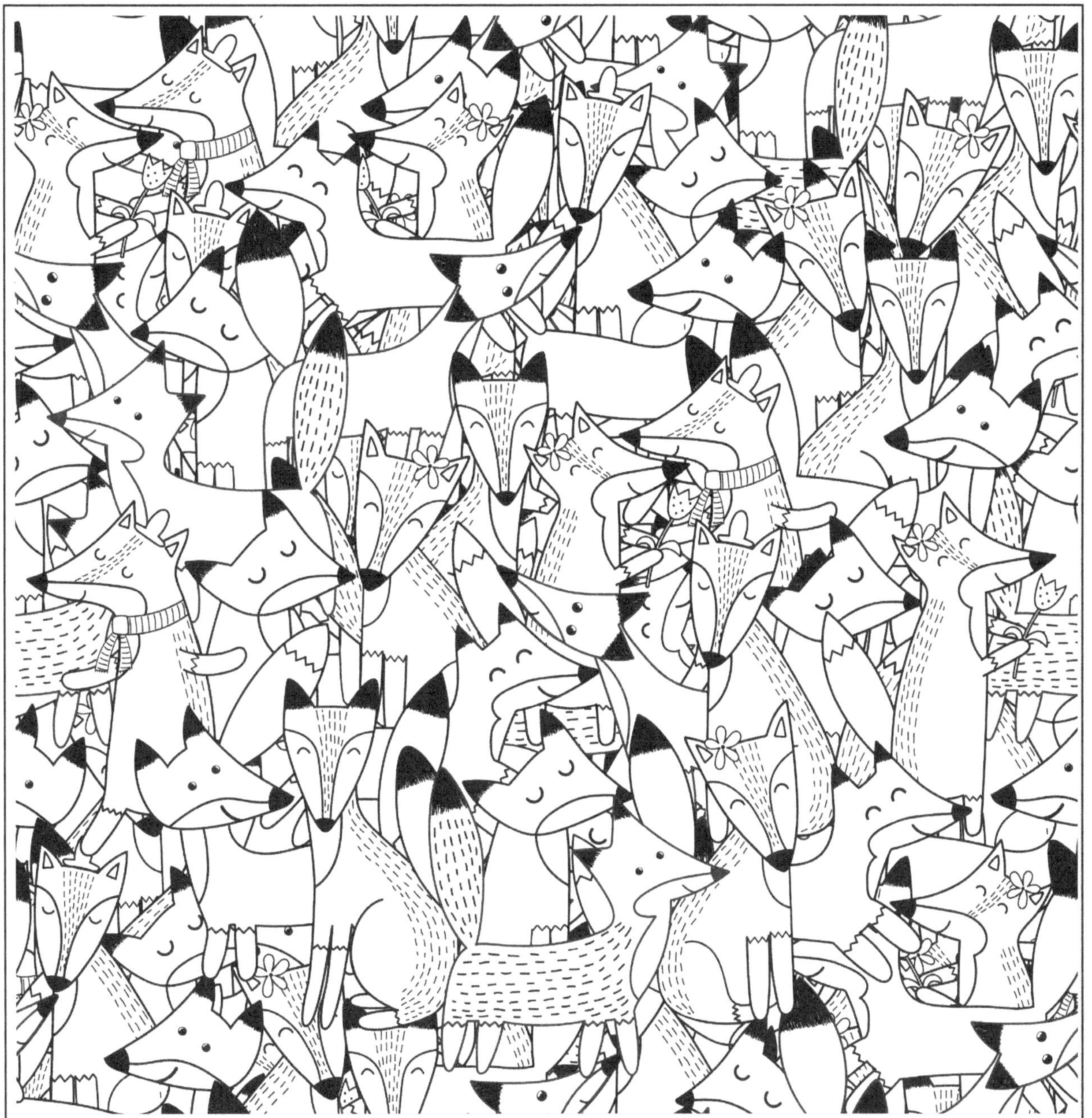

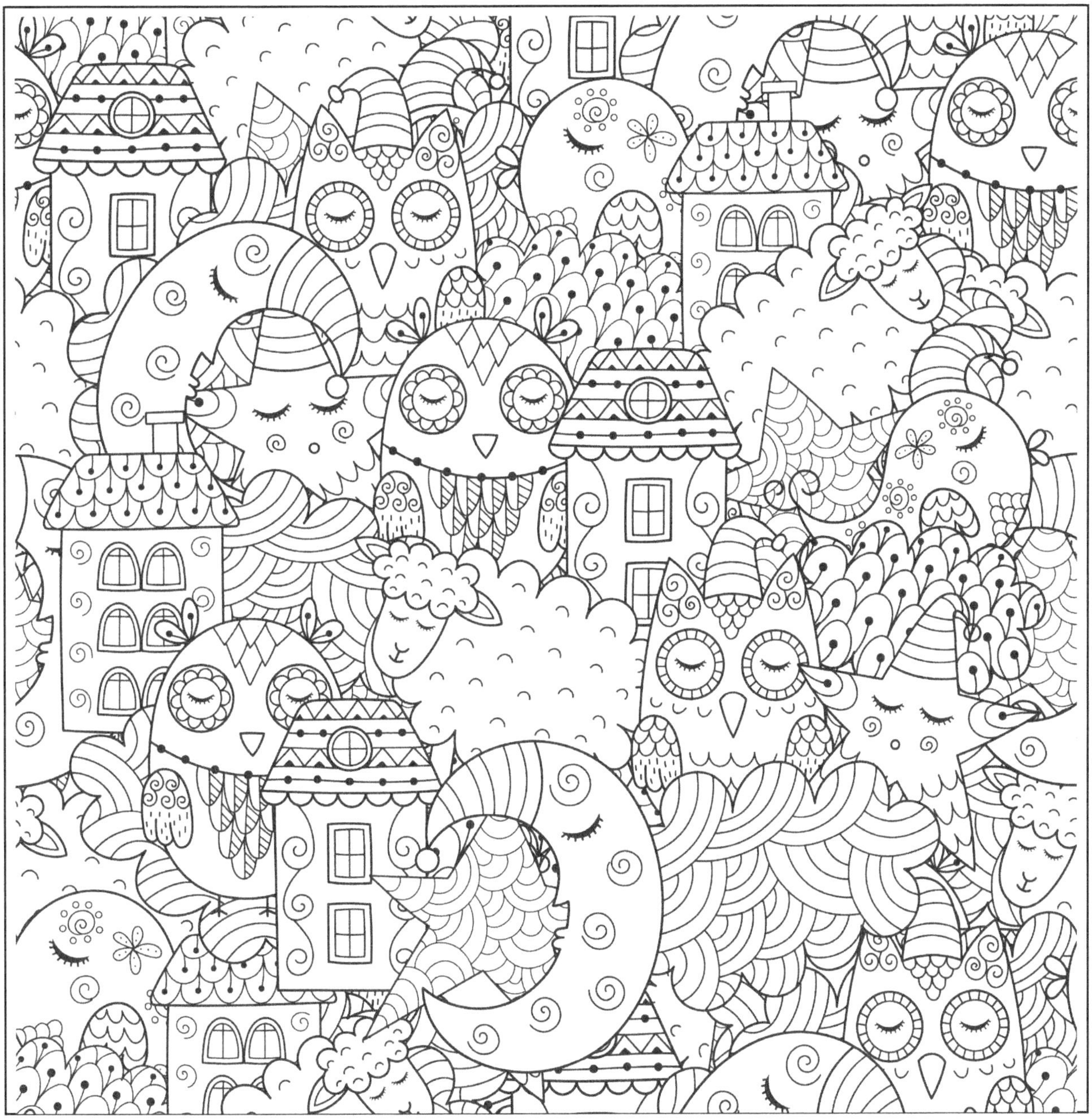

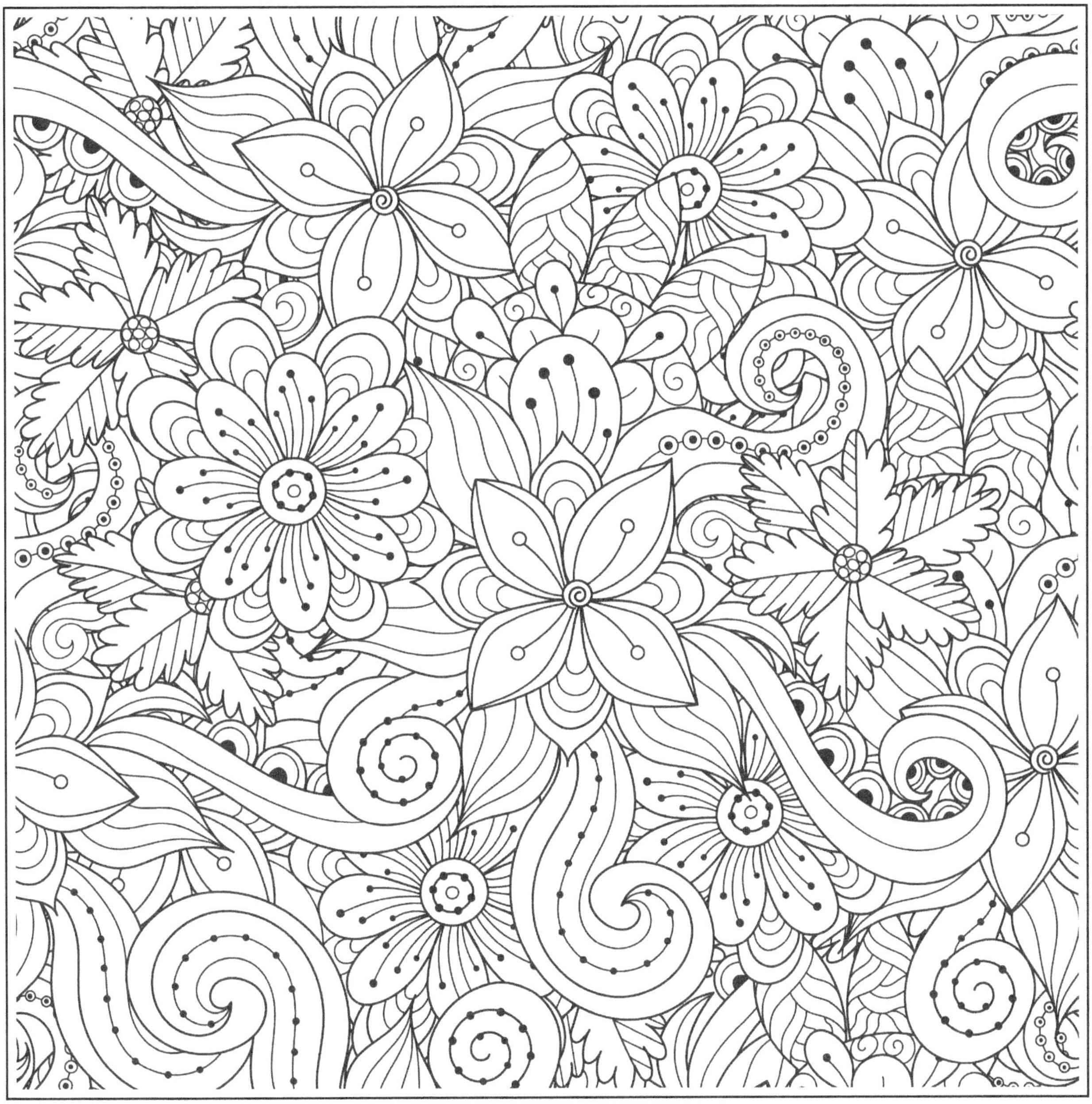

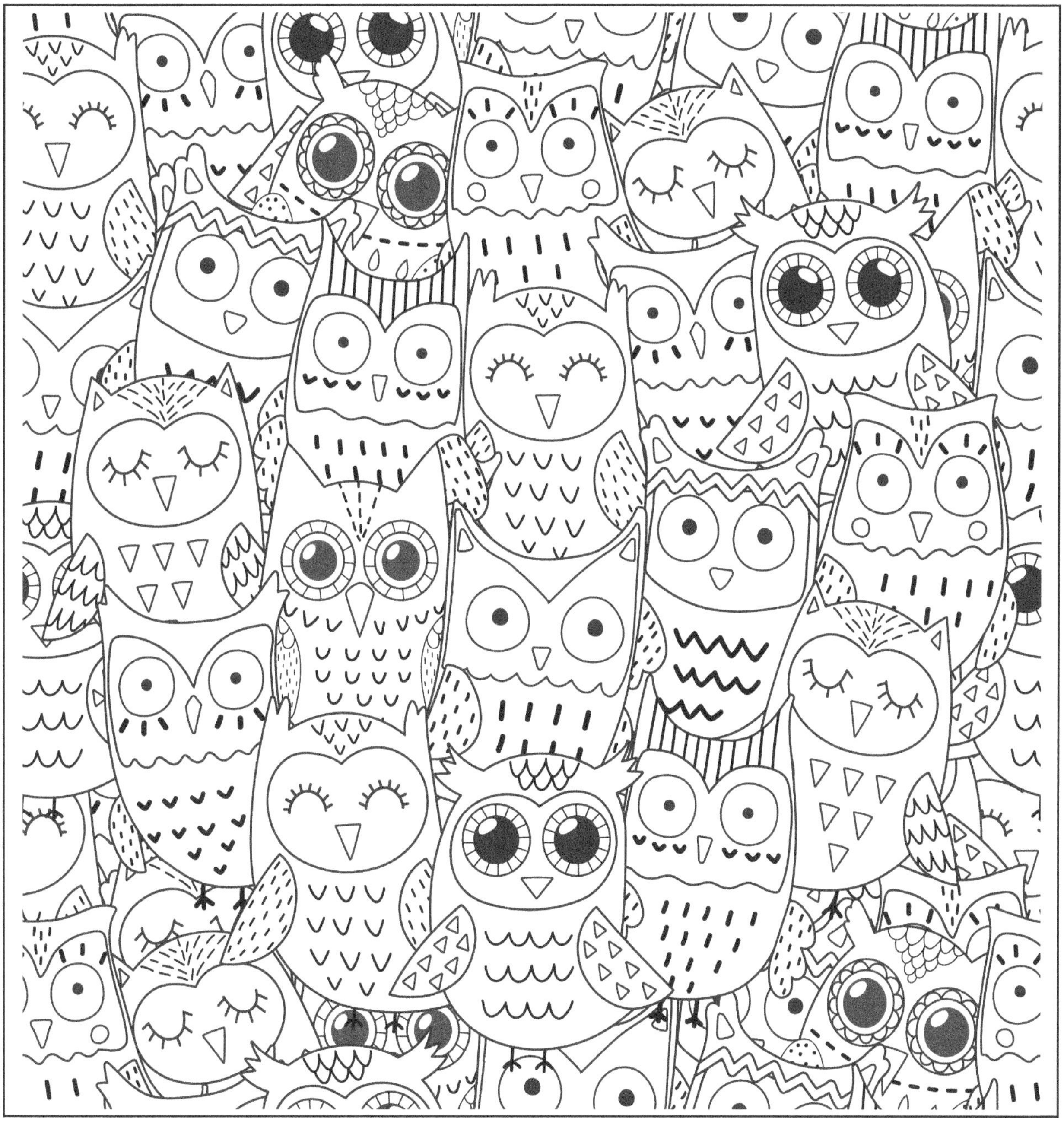

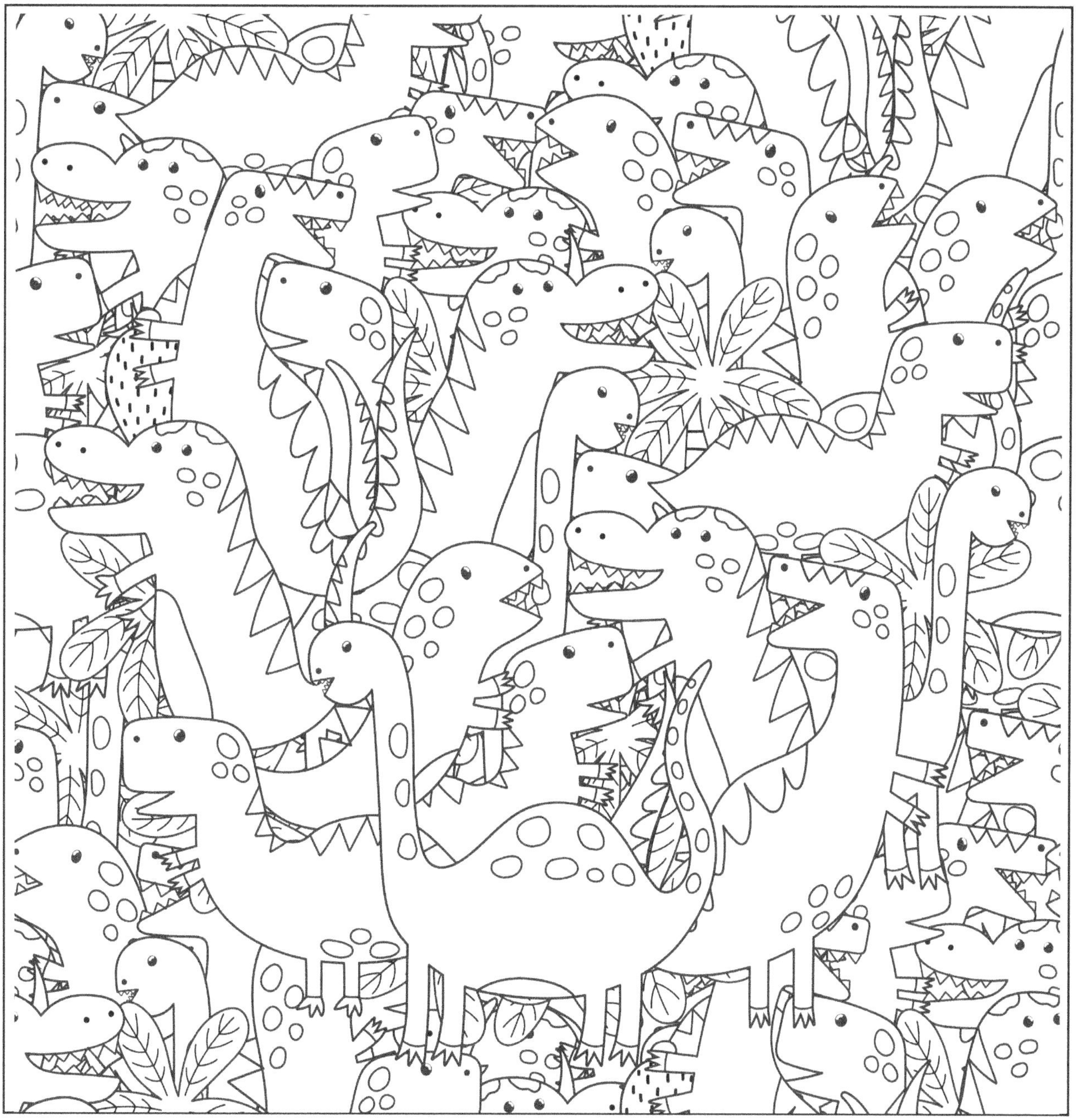

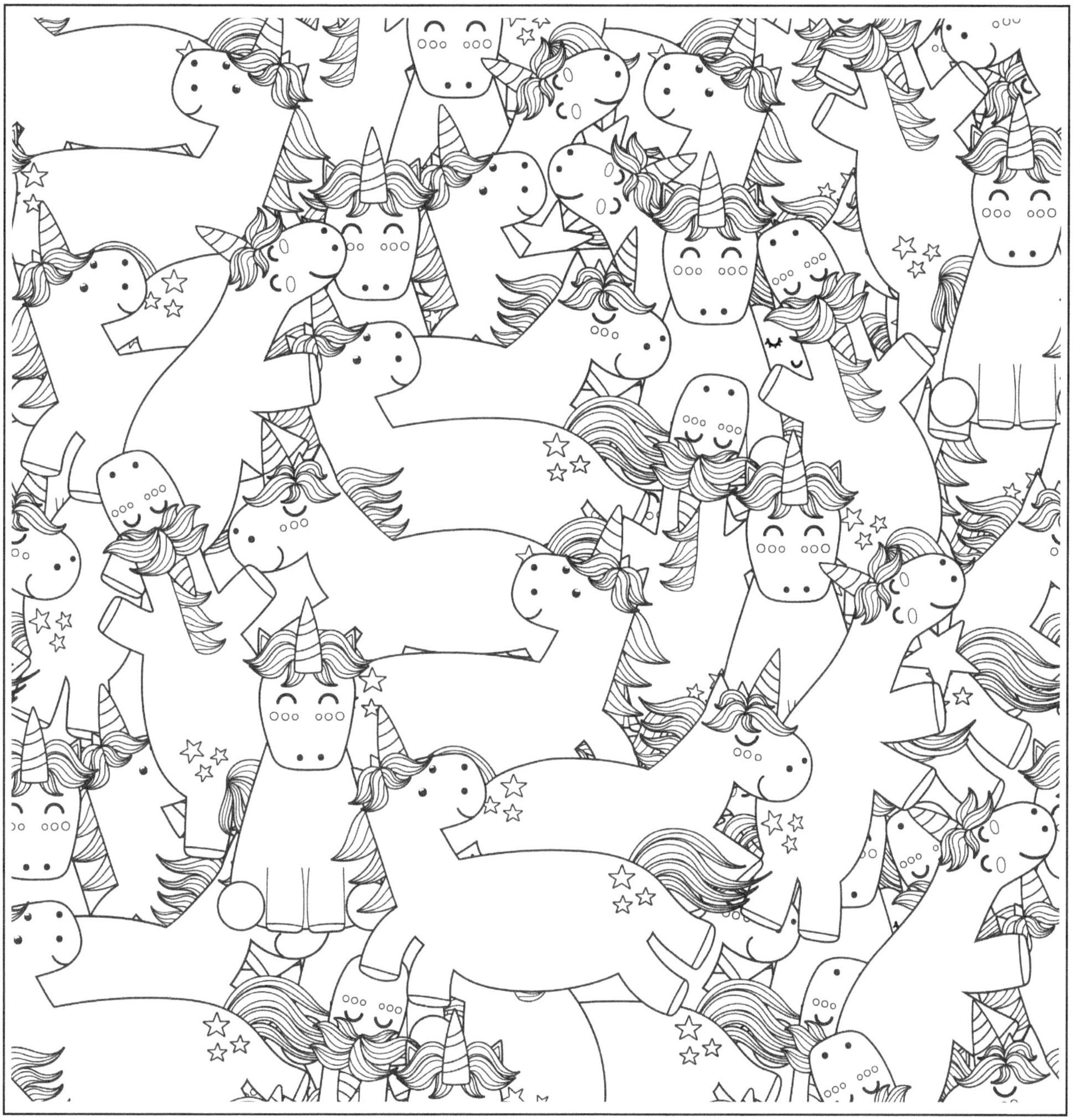

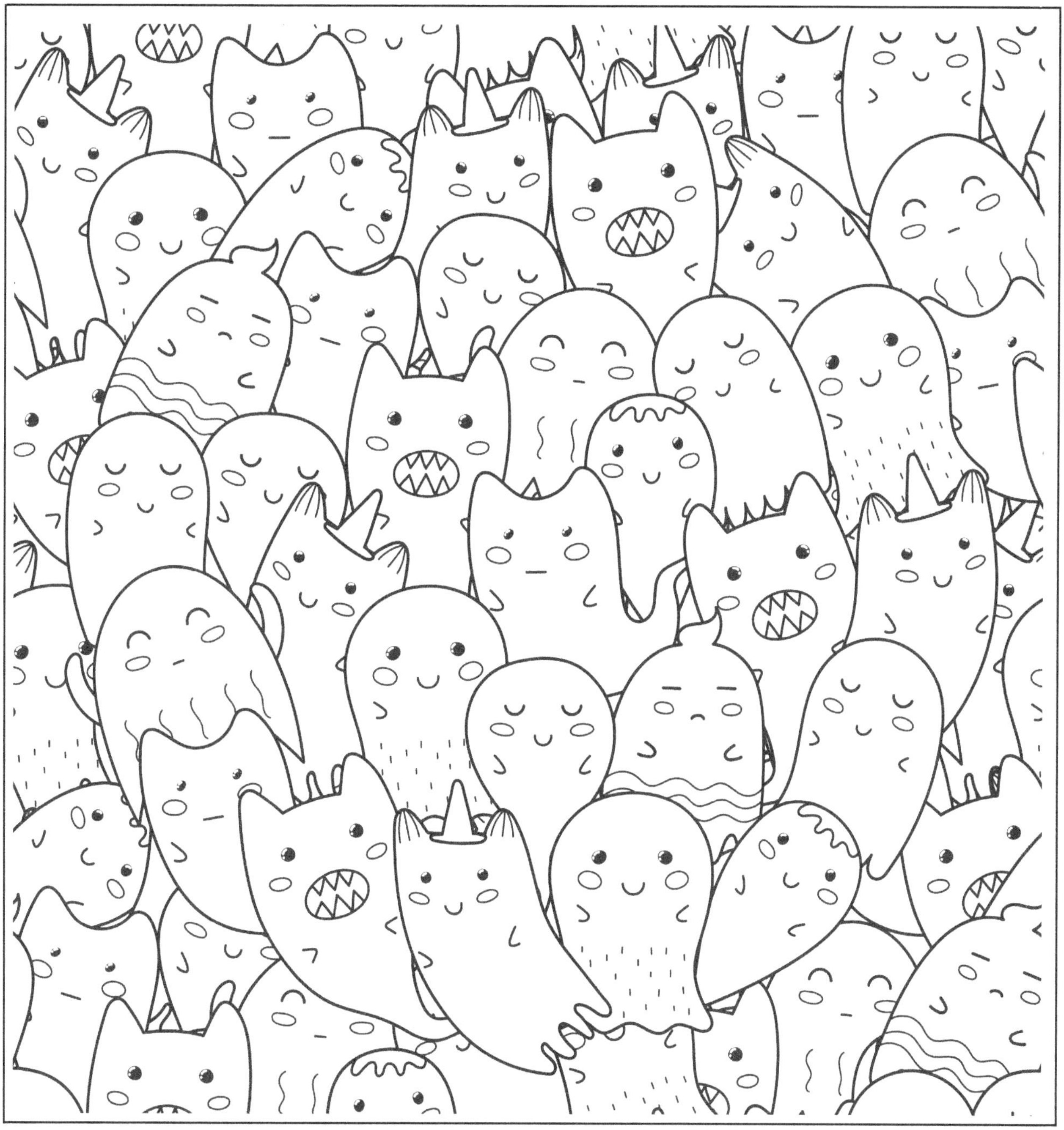

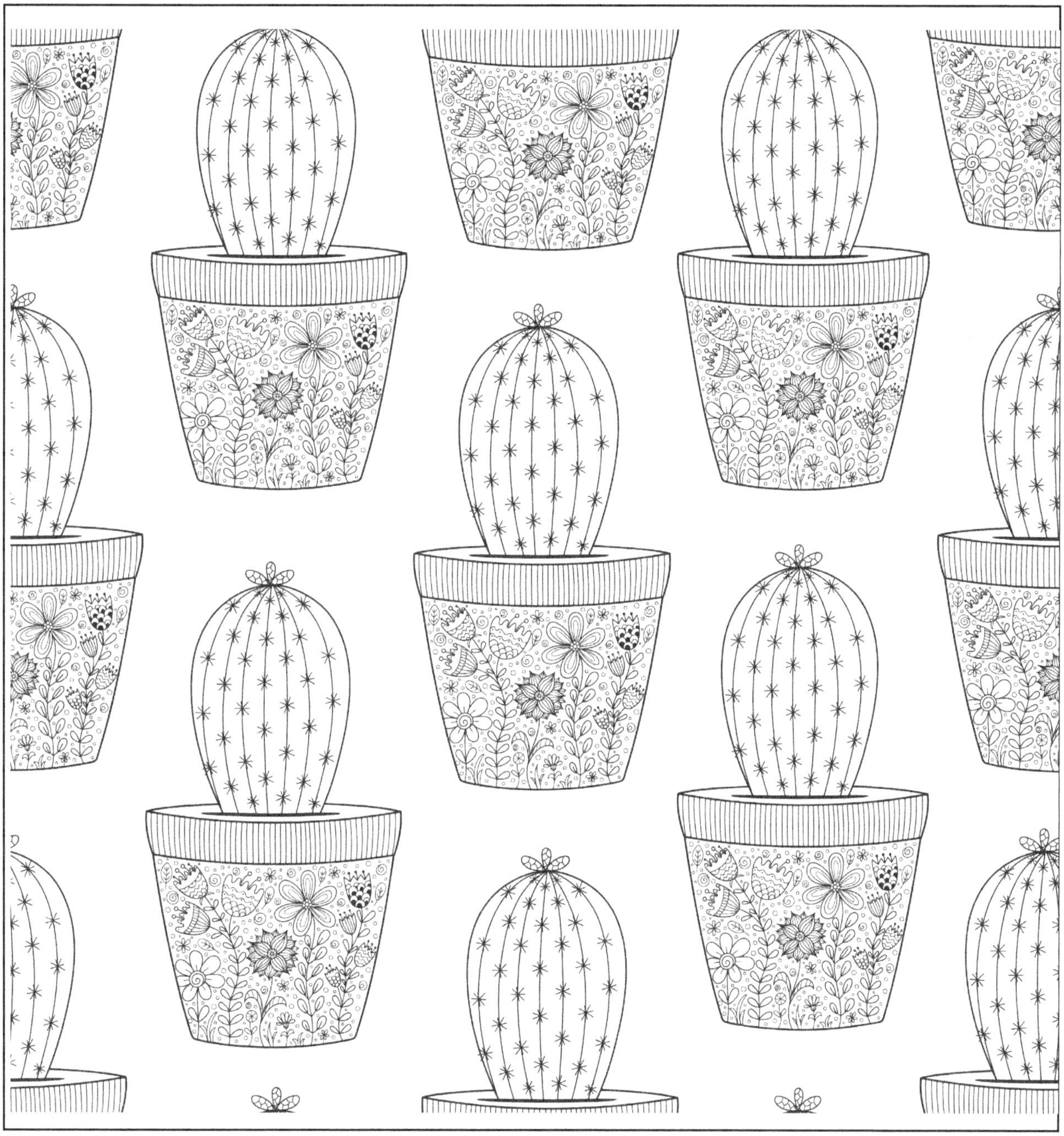

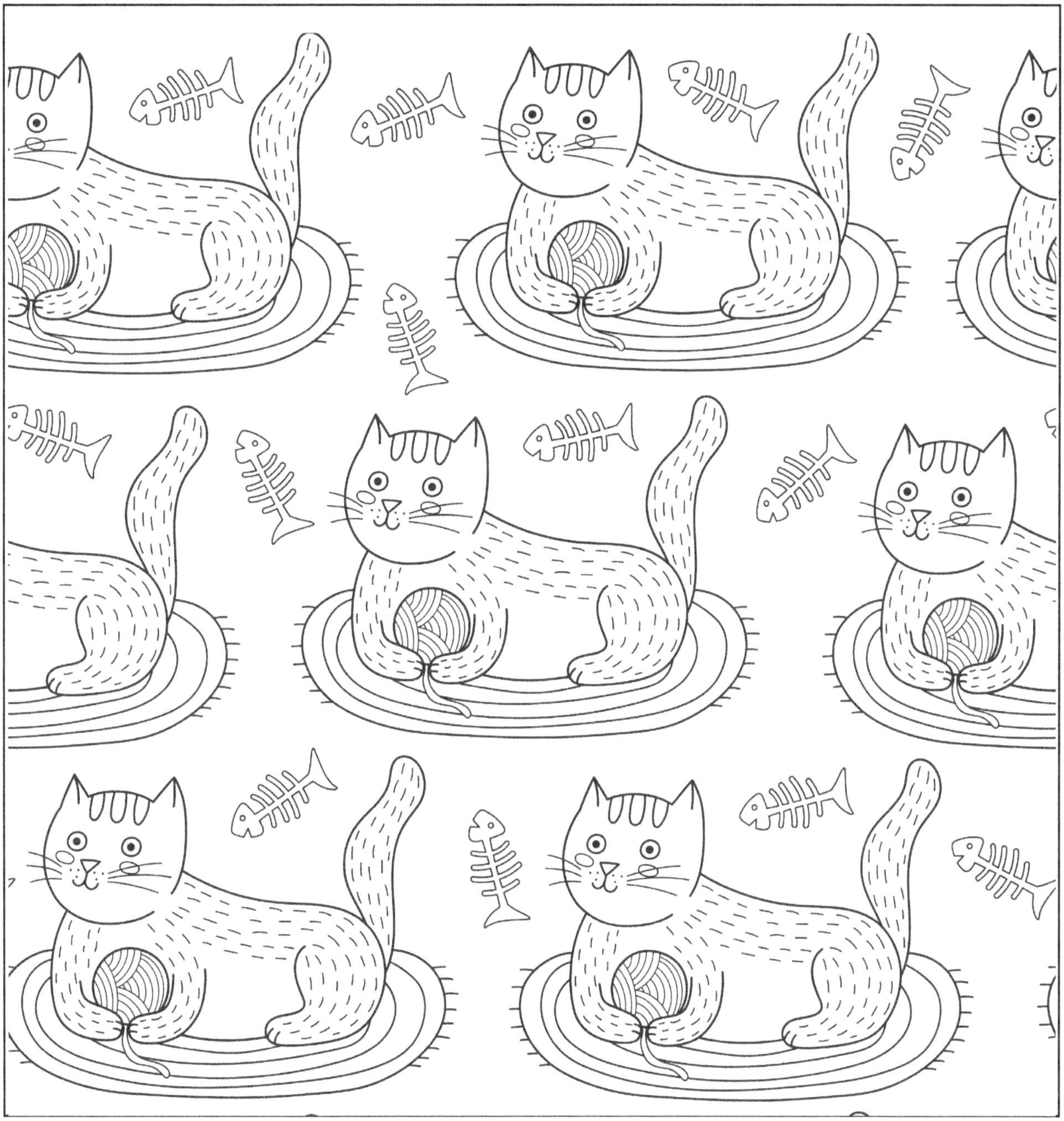

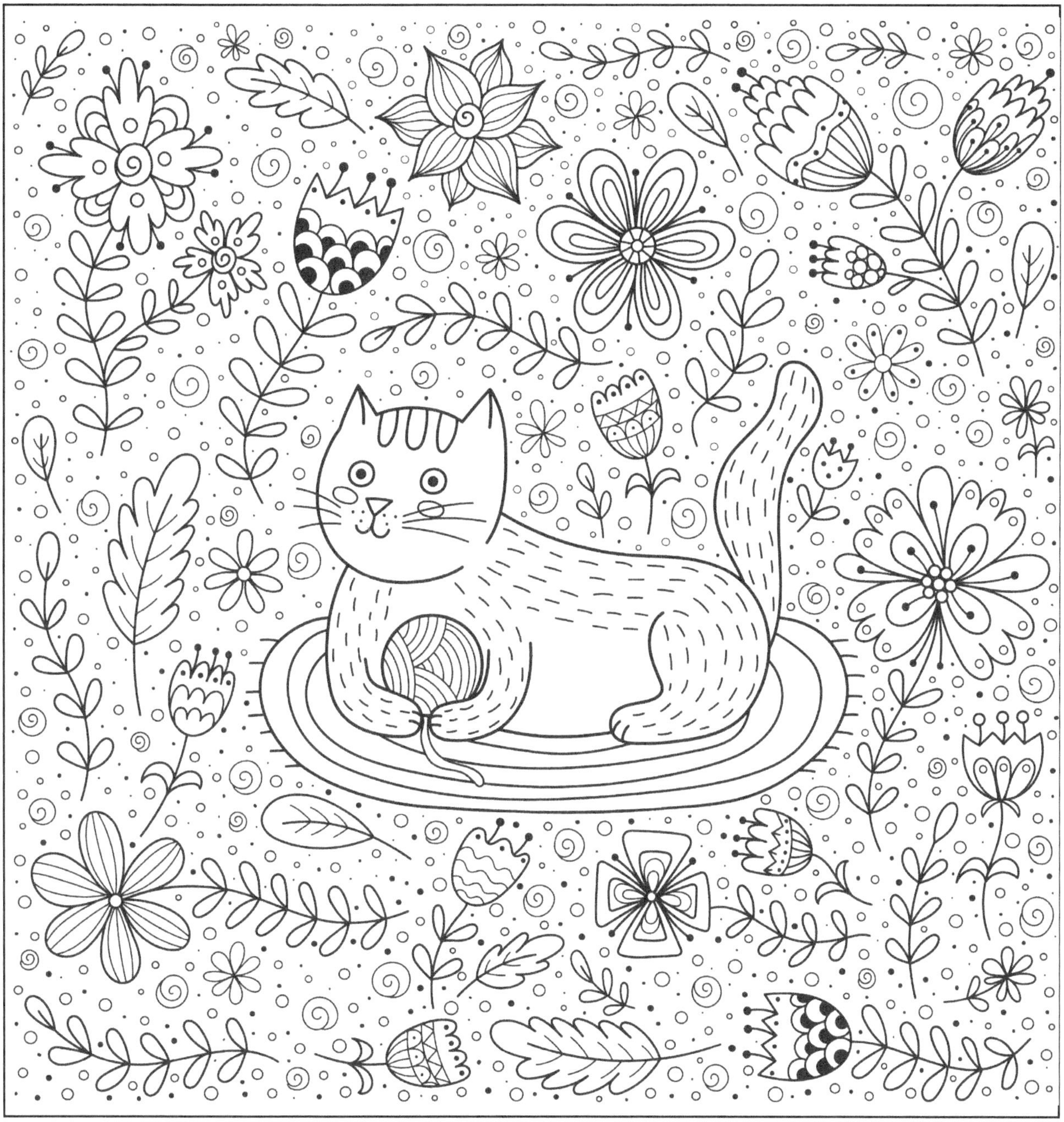

www.ingramcontent.com/pod-product-compliance
Lightning Source LLC
Chambersburg PA
CBHW081500220526
45466CB00008B/2734
9781687772084